Searchlight
BOOKS™

What
Can We
Learn from Early
Civilizations?

Tools and Treasures of the Ancient Maya

Matt Doeden

Lerner Publications Company
Minneapolis

Lerner Publications Company
A division of Lerner Publishing Group, Inc.
241 First Avenue North
Minneapolis, MN 55401 U.S.A.

For reading levels and more information, look up this title at www.lernerbooks.com.

Library of Congress Cataloging-in-Publication Data

Doeden, Matt.
    Tools and treasures of the ancient Maya / by Matt Doeden.
        pages   cm. — (Searchlight books™ : what can we learn from early civilizations?)
    Includes index.
    ISBN 978–1–4677–1431–0 (lib. bdg. : alk. paper)
    ISBN 978–1–4677–2509–5 (e-Book)
    1. Mayas—Juvenile literature. I. Title.
    F1435.D64 2014
    972.81—dc23   2013020472

Manufactured in the United States of America
1 – PC – 12/31/13

Contents

Chapter 1

THE ANCIENT MAYA

More than one thousand years ago, the Maya civilization thrived in Mesoamerica. This region includes Central America and the southern part of Mexico.

These are ruins of a Maya city. Where are the cities of the Maya found?

The Maya culture was rich and diverse. Its people were skilled farmers and brave warriors. They built huge stone temples. They honored their gods, offered sacrifices, and studied astronomy at the temples. The Maya were fascinated with time. They studied the stars and the planets. They created calendars that stretched for thousands of years. And many Maya tools, temples, and works of art have survived. These tools and treasures tell us many things about this ancient culture.

These people are searching the burial site of a Maya leader.

Rise and Fall

We don't know just when the Maya civilization began.
Some think it started as long ago as 2600 BCE.
Others think it began about nine hundred years later.

We learn about the ancient
Maya culture through their
paintings and stone carvings.

The Maya developed at the same time as many other Mesoamerican cultures. These cultures include the Olmec people and the people of Teotihuacán city. Some think the Maya culture came from the Olmec culture. The Olmec was the first major civilization in the region.

This is an Olmec head. The Olmec carved these giant heads out of large boulders and placed them near their cities.

The Maya were the only people in Mesoamerica to live mainly in the jungle. Living and farming in the jungle was difficult. But the Maya people learned how to use what the jungle had to offer. The Maya used plants and animals for food and medicine.

The jungle is always warm and damp. It is hard to farm there because the tall trees shade crops from the sunlight they need.

The Maya became expert farmers. They built flat terraces on mountain slopes for farming. They also cleared jungle growth to make farm fields. They grew corn, called maize, and other crops on their rich farms.

These modern farmers in Guatemala grow crops on terraces, just like the ancient Maya.

The Maya reached the height of their power from about 250 CE to 900 CE. The ancient Maya civilization was divided into city-states. These city-states spread across Mesoamerica. Then the Maya suddenly left their cities. The Maya people survived. But their civilization crumbled. No one knows why.

These ancient Maya people watch a sporting event in their city.

Maya Homeland

Ancient Maya Civilization

○ City

Miles
0   50   100   150

0   100   200
Kilometers

GULF OF MEXICO

Chichén Itzá ○

Uxmal ○   Tulum ○

N

MEXICO

Xunantunich ○

Tikal ○

Caracol ○

BELIZE

CARIBBEAN SEA

GUATEMALA   HONDURAS

○ Copán

EL SALVADOR

PACIFIC OCEAN

Chapter 2

DAILY LIFE

Maya life was focused on work, family, and religion. Maya people farmed the land. They worshipped their gods at temples. The Maya created fine crafts and works of art. Some Maya could even read and write.

The Maya used these tools to grind the corn they grew on their farms. From what class did Maya farmers come?

Classes

The daily life of a Maya depended on class. There were several classes in Maya society. Most Maya were common people. Some were nobles or priests. And others were slaves.

The common Maya people included architects, stonecutters, and carpenters. But most common Maya were farmers. The men worked in the fields to raise maize, beans, and other crops. The men also hunted for meat.

Servants help a priest prepare for a ceremony.

Most women usually stayed in the home. They fixed meals and wove clothing. Women also sometimes helped in the fields.

Common people dressed simply. Men covered themselves with loincloths. Women wore simple woven dresses or skirts.

This stone statue shows a woman weaving clothing.

Nobles led very different lives from the common Maya. Each city-state had nobles and a king. Together they ruled the people of the city-state.

Nobles dressed in decorated clothing. They wore jewelry made from a stone called jade. Many also had tattoos. Tattoos often showed animals or gods.

Two nobles in this stone carving wear elaborate headdresses and jewelry.

Priests were another powerful class. Nobles may have ruled. But priests made the decisions. They chose when to plant and harvest. They even chose when to sacrifice people to their gods! Maya priests were also astronomers. They tracked the movements of the planets and stars.

This ancient Maya vase shows a priest in a ceremonial outfit.

The Maya sometimes captured enemies in battle. These people became slaves. Orphans or people caught stealing also became slaves. They had to work for no pay. Many were sacrificed to the Maya gods.

This is a jade statue of a servant.

Communication

Maya city-states remained in close contact. A system of roads connected their cities. The Maya people all spoke similar languages. More than twenty different Mayan languages are still spoken.

THE MAYA BUILT ROADS THROUGH THE JUNGLE. SOME OF THEM STILL SURVIVE NEAR THE RUINS.

The Maya also had a form of writing. This written language was made up of eight hundred pictures. The pictures included people, animals, and gods. Each picture stood for a sound. The Maya combined the pictures to create words and sentences. The Maya wrote on stone and an early form of paper.

This pillar has Maya writing on it.

Religion

Religion was very important to the Maya. They worshipped many gods of nature. Gods of the sun, rain, and of corn were just a few. The Maya believed that these gods controlled the weather, harvests, and even earthquakes. The Maya needed to keep the gods happy.

This is a statue of the Maya corn god.

The Maya built huge temples to the gods. The temples were shaped like pyramids. The Maya gave the gods offerings. They gave the gods food, drink, and animals. But blood was the most important offering given to the gods. Sometimes humans were sacrificed to keep the gods happy.

The Maya would offer sacrifices to their gods on the altar at the top of temples like this one.

Calendars

The Maya created complex calendars. They used their calendars for farming and religion. The calendars also tracked other important Maya events. The Long Count calendar stretched for thousands of years. The Calendar Round was shorter. It lasted 52 years.

Maya calendars were carved on huge pieces of stone.

Chapter 3

THE CULTURE OF THE MAYA

The Maya had a rich culture. They studied science and medicine. They built great cities and amazing stone temples. Some of these temples are still standing!

The Maya built many things. What was one thing the Maya built?

Arts and Crafts

The Maya valued their arts and crafts. Painters created large murals on buildings. They showed different parts of Maya life. They also show the colorful clothing worn by the Maya.

This mural decorates a wall of the oldest known Maya royal tomb.

Sculptors carved figures into stone. Some figures were carved on the sides of buildings. The figures stood out from flat stone backgrounds. Some sculptures were made from large rocks or columns of stone. Animals, Maya leaders, and gods were common subjects.

Sculptors carved figures to decorate the temples and the homes of the nobles.

The Maya also made colorful, folding books. These books are called codices. They were written on an early form of paper. One book is the seventy-eight-page Dresden Codex. It is filled with detailed writing and pictures.

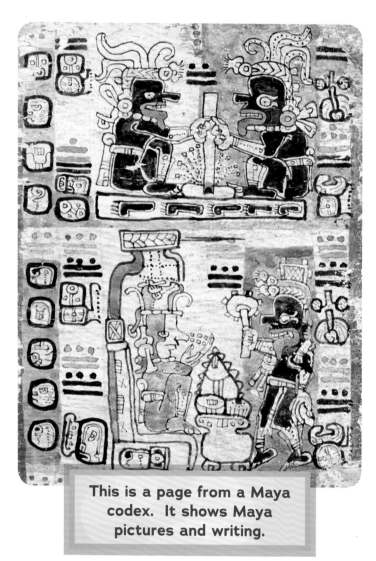

This is a page from a Maya codex. It shows Maya pictures and writing.

Maya crafts were finely made. The Maya people carved jade into jewelry, masks, and figures. The Maya created stone tools and weapons. The people spun brightly colored cotton cloth. And they made fine, painted pottery.

The Maya carved jade masks like this one for a noble who had died.

Architecture

The Maya were also skilled builders. Common people lived in simple one-story homes. They were built of wood, thatch, and adobe. Nobles lived in large stone palaces. Each palace had several buildings with different levels. Many had large, open courtyards.

Common people had open spaces near their homes to cook their food outside.

A stone temple stood at the center of each city. Many Maya temples still stand after more than one thousand years! Most Maya temples were pyramid-shaped. Steep staircases led to the top of the temples. Many were built to line up with the sun, the moon, or other planets and stars.

This Maya temple in Chichén Itzá lines up with the sunset.

Sports

The Maya played a ball game to honor the Maya gods. The Maya built large ball courts near some temples. The ball game was played in teams. Each team worked to hit a small ball through a stone ring. The exact rules of the game are not known. But sometimes the losers were sacrificed to the gods!

In Maya ball games, players tried to get a heavy rubber ball through a tiny hoop.

The Maya Creation Story

The Maya told many stories. Each explained a natural event or taught a lesson. The Maya creation story explained how the Maya thought gods created the world.

The world started in darkness. There was only an ancient ocean and the sky. Then the god Huracán made light appear. He also created land from the sea. Next, the gods of nature made plants and animals. The world they created was very beautiful. But the gods wanted more. They wanted people to worship them.

The gods first made people out of mud. But these people only melted. Next, the gods made people out of wood. But these people had no spirit. Finally, the gods made people out of corn dough. These people were the ancient ancestors of modern people.

Chapter 4

THE FATE OF THE MAYA

The Maya were at their height of power from about 250 until 900. Then their civilization collapsed. What happened?

The Maya warrior statue stands for strength. But the Maya civilization didn't last forever. When did it end?

The Collapse

Sometime around 900, the busy Maya cities were deserted. The Maya people left their homes in the jungle. The temples fell to ruin. No one knows exactly why.

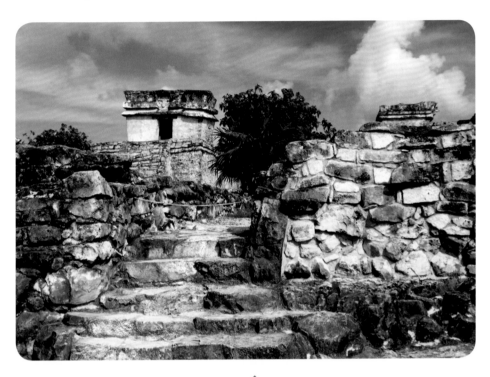

THESE ARE RUINS FROM
A MAYA CITY IN MEXICO.

Scientists do have some ideas. The Maya were very successful. Their population had soared. They may not have been able to feed everyone in the cities. Scientists also think that Mesoamerica had a long drought around this time. The land grew dry and the crops may have failed. The people may not have had enough food.

Corn and other crops cannot grow if they do not get enough rain. The ancient Maya may have left their cities if their corn died.

But some Maya cities in the far north survived. They lasted until the early 1500s, when Spanish explorers came to the region. The Spanish explorers conquered the Maya and other native cultures. The age of Maya rule was truly over.

Pedro de Alvarado, a Spanish explorer, conquered the Maya in Guatemala.

Maya People Today

The great Maya civilization ended. But its people and their culture did not die out. More than 6 million Maya people live in Mexico, Guatemala, and Belize. Much of their culture has changed. But some Maya try to hold on to their old ways. They speak Mayan languages. They remember the Maya gods.

A young Maya girl listens in class. Many Maya still live near their ancestors' homes.

Many Maya temples still stand. The ruins of Chichén Itzá, Copán, and Caracol attract tourists from around the world. These ancient temples remind modern Maya people of the once-great civilization that rose out of the jungle.

Tourists visit a Maya temple in Chichén Itzá, Mexico.

Glossary

adobe: a building material made from clay, sand, water, and plant material

astronomy: the study of the sun, moon, stars, and other objects in outer space

city-state: a self-governing city and the lands it controls

civilization: a large society in which people share a common government and culture

codex: an ancient book

conquer: to take over a land by force

loincloth: a single piece of cloth wrapped around the hips

mural: a painting or other work of art applied directly to a wall

noble: a person of high rank in a society

offering: something that is given up to honor a god

sacrifice: to kill an animal or a person as an offering to a god

sculpture: a carving made out of stone or wood

temple: a building that is used to worship a god or gods

terrace: a flattened area on a slope, such as a mountainside

thatch: a roof that is made of straw or reeds

Learn More about the Ancient Maya

Books

Doeden, Matt. *Tools and Treasure of Ancient Greece.* Minneapolis: Lerner Publications, 2014. Have you seen ancient Greek sculptures? Do you wonder about this civilization? Find out all about it in this book.

Ollhoff, Jim. *Mayan and Aztec Mythology.* Edina, MN: Abdo Publishing, 2012. Find out more about Maya gods and the ancient religion of the Maya.

Pipe, Jim. *Mysteries of the Mayan Calendar.* New York: Crabtree, 2013. Learn about the Maya culture and the calendars these ancient people created.

Websites

Highlights Kids—Exploring the Ancient Civilization of the Maya
http://www.highlightskids.com/stories/exploring-ancient-civilization
-maya
Do you wonder what it is like to explore an ancient Maya temple? Visit this site to read what it is like to visit Chichén Itzá.

Mayan Kids
http://www.mayankids.com
Find out many things about Maya culture and this ancient civilization.

National Geographic—Mysteries of the Maya
http://ngm.nationalgeographic.com/2008/08/maya-issue
/table-of-contents
Visit this site to see a gallery of Maya art, buildings, and sculpture. You can also check out fifteen Maya sites using a map.

LERNER
e
SOURCE

Expand learning beyond the printed book. Download free, complementary educational resources for this book from our website, www.lernerresource.com.

Index

Photo Acknowledgments

The images in this book are used with the permission of: © Danny Lehman/CORBIS, p. 4; © Daniel LeClair/REUTERS/CORBIS, p. 5; © Gianni Dagli Orti/Corbis, p. 6; © Adalberto Rios Szalay/Sexto Sol/Getty Images, p. 7; © Frans Lanting/CORBIS, p. 8; © Richard Wareham Fotografie/Alamy, p. 9; © Peter E. Spier/National Geographic/Getty Images, p. 10; © Laura Westland/Independent Picture Services, p. 11; © Michael Freeman/Alamy, p. 12; © G. DAGLI ORTI/De Agostini/Getty Images, pp. 13, 17, 31 (top); © Werner Forman/Corbis, pp. 14, 15; © Gianni Dagli Orti/The Art Archive at Art Resource, NY, pp. 16, 28, 35; © Erich Lessing/Art Resource, NY, pp. 18, 27; © Charles & Josette Lenars/CORBIS, p. 19; © Danita Delimont/Alamy, p. 20; © Joseph Calev/Dreamstime.com, p. 21; © Stephen Sweet/Dreamstime.com, p. 22; © Terry W. Rutledge/National Geographic/Getty Images, p. 23; © Kenneth Garrett/National Geographic/Getty Images, p. 24; © Macduff Everton/CORBIS, p. 25; © The Bridgeman Art Library/Getty Images, p. 26; © Patryk Kosmider/Dreamstime.com, p. 29; © A.A.M. Van der Heyden/Independent Picture Service, p. 30; © Seanyu/Dreamstime.com, p. 31 (bottom); © Bertrand Gardel/Hemis/Corbis, p. 32; © Jannis Werner/Dreamstime.com, p. 33; © iStockphoto.com/dhughes9, p. 34; © GILLARDI Jacques/Getty Images, p. 36; © Melvyn Longhurst/Alamy, p. 37.

Front Cover: © G. DAGLI ORTI/De Agostini/Getty Images.

Main body text set in Adrianna Regular 14/20
Typeface provided by Chank